Alphabet Adventures

By Rosemary Sunday
Illustrated by Geri Livingston

Based on characters originated by Lyn Wendon

Published by Letterland International Ltd
Barton, Cambridge, CB23 7AY, UK
Tel: +44 (0)870 766 2629
Fax: +44 (0)1223 264126
Email: info@letterland.com

www.letterland.com

© Letterland International 2007
12 11 10 9 8 7 6 5 4 3

ISBN: 978-1-86209-242-6
Product Code: T11

First published 1996. This new edition published 2003, reprinted 2006.
LETTERLAND® is a registered trademark of Lyn Wendon,
The right of Lyn Wendon to be identified as the author of this work has been asserted in
accordance with Sections 77 and 78 of the Copyright, Designs & Patents Act 1988

British Library Cataloguing in Publication Data
A catalogue record for this book is available from the British Library

Designed by Susi Martin

Contents

Annie Apple

Bouncy Ben

Clever Cat

Dippy Duck

Eddy Elephant

Zig Zag Zebra

Yellow Yo-yo Man

Fix-it Max

About this Book

Letterland is a special place where all the Letterland characters live and, like all special places, it's great fun to visit. But there's more to Letterland than just having fun, because each Letterlander acts like a memory cue, helping children to make instant links between a letter shape and its sound – one of the key skills a child needs in order to become a successful reader!

The key to success lies in Letterland's special 'sound trick'. By just *starting* to say a character's name, for example, 'a…' for Annie Apple, or 'fff…' for Firefighter Fred, a child automatically says the correct letter sound. It's that simple!

There are lots of ways you can enjoy this book with your child to help them on the road to reading. Here are a few suggestions:

- Look at the pictures together, read the poems and talk about all the fun things the Letterlanders are doing and the exciting places they visit – the beach, the jungle, the mountain tops, the ocean deeps, even outer space!

- Find all 26 Letterlanders in each scene. Some characters may be easier to spot than others!

Walter Walrus

Vicky Violet

Uppy Umbrella

Talking Tess

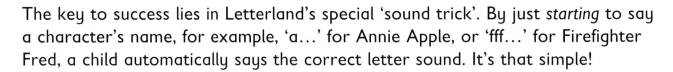
Sammy Snake

Firefighter Fred

Golden Girl

Harry Hat Man

Impy Ink

Jumping Jim

Kicking King

- Flip through the pages finding the same Letterlander in each scene. Look for things that begin with that character's sound and talk about them, so that the 'target sound' is repeated again and again. For example:

  "Look! **B**ouncy **B**en has just **b**aked some **b**uns. Here's **B**ouncy **B**en at the **b**each, playing with his **b**all. Now **B**ouncy **B**en is racing in a **b**oat made from a **b**arrel. And here's **B**ouncy **B**en being **B**atman!"

  Sharp eyes will find nearby objects that begin with a character's sound, such as a fountain behind Firefighter Fred, a lighthouse behind Lucy Lamp Light, and a huge whale behind Walter Walrus.

Lucy Lamp Light

- Try playing a game using this book along with the *Letterland First Reading Flashcards*. Shuffle the cards and take turns to pick one card at a time. Say the name of the Letterlander on the front of the card, then look for that Letterlander in one of the scenes. Also try to find something that begins with that character's sound. Play it again using the plain letter side of the cards.

Munching Mike

- Finally, take up the challenge of Quarrelsome Queen's Questions which you'll find at the back of the book on page 30.

Red Robot   **Quarrelsome Queen**

Peter Puppy

Oscar Orange

Noisy Nick

Café Society

It's a sunny day in Letterland Square.
See all the Letterlanders eating there.
Bouncy Ben has been baking today.
But why is Dippy Duck flying away?

CAFÉ

PIZZA

7

Garden Capers

In Letterland garden all good things grow.
See Red Robot rake and Munching Mike mow.
Vicky has found lots of vegetables to eat.
What's in that basket by her feet?

8

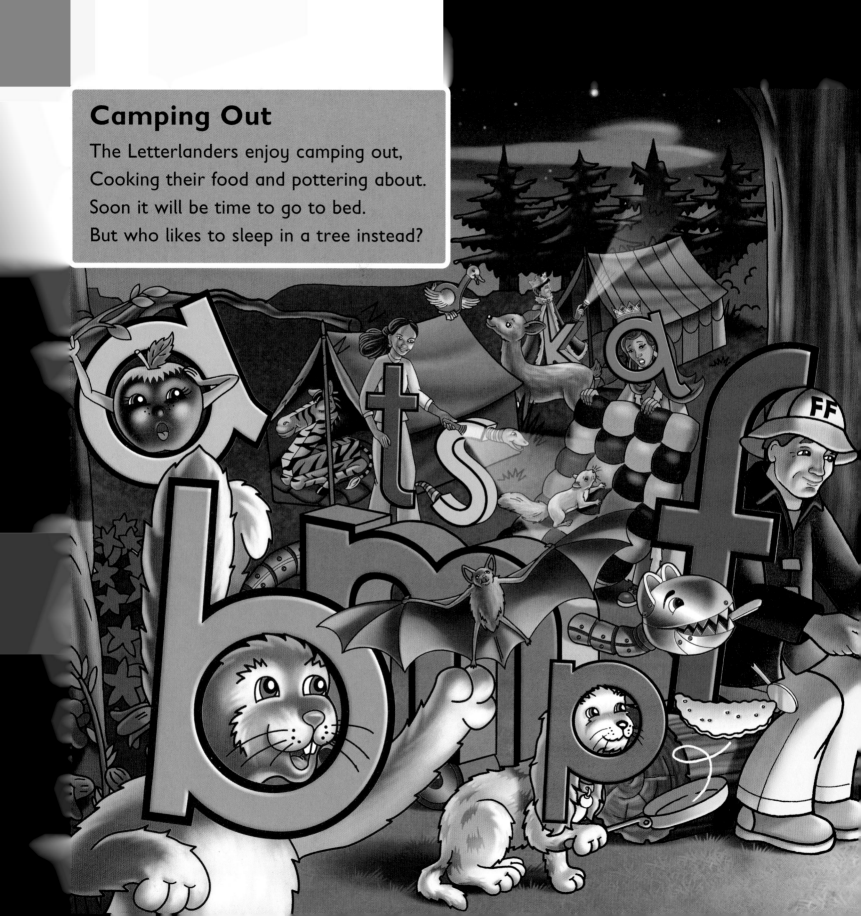

Camping Out

The Letterlanders enjoy camping out,
Cooking their food and pottering about.
Soon it will be time to go to bed.
But who likes to sleep in a tree instead?

Party Time

It's party time here in Letterland.
Fred and Vicky join in the band.
Who's that leaping out of the cake,
Causing the queen to quiver and quake?

Splish, Splash, Splosh!

Into the water everyone dashes.
Now they're all in, everyone splashes!
Who will get rusty if he swims in his ring?
Ask Clever Cat – she knows everything!

14

Down in the Deep Blue Sea

Deep underwater there's so much to see –
All sorts of creatures, and treasure, and me!
Can you spot me in front of the whale,
With my two white tusks and swishy tail?

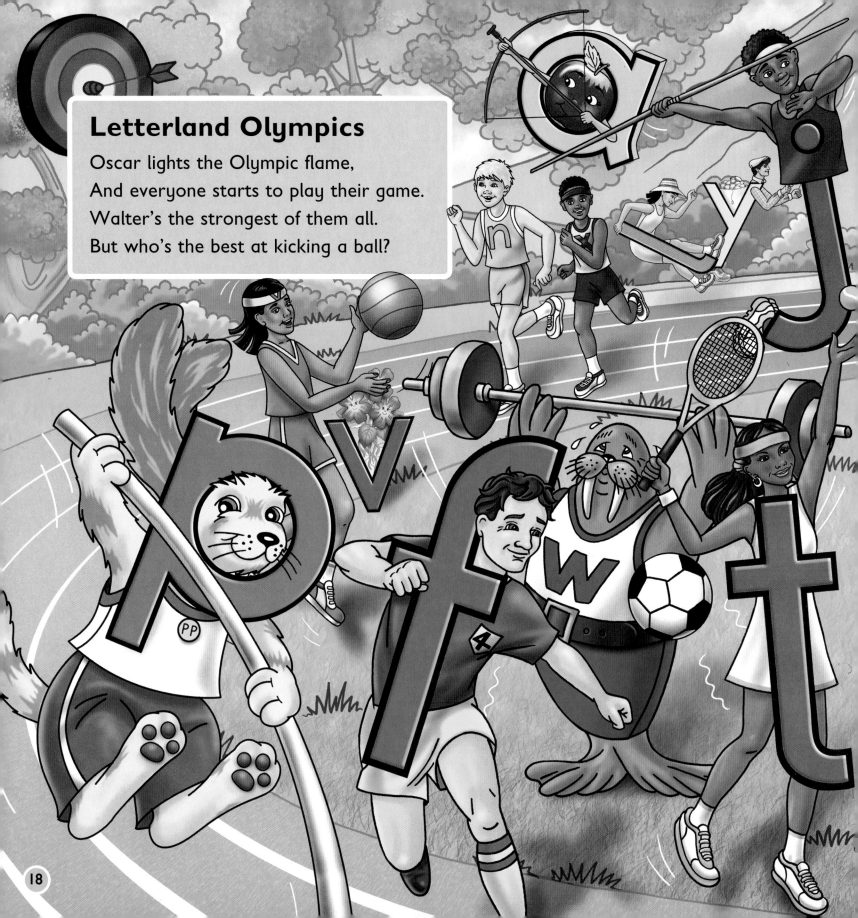

Letterland Olympics

Oscar lights the Olympic flame,
And everyone starts to play their game.
Walter's the strongest of them all.
But who's the best at kicking a ball?

LETTERLAND OLYMPIC GAMES

19

It's All Go in the Snow!

The Letterland friends are enjoying the snow.
See who's skiing – just look at them go!
Who's fallen over as his friends whizz by?
And who's that gliding high in the sky?

High Jinks in the Jungle

Everyone's gone to the jungle today.
And all the animals have come out to play.
Who's found a nice cool watery spot?
And who's that chasing Red Robot?

23

Rip-Roaring Racing

Who will win the Letterland race?
Is it Impy Ink with a smile on his face?
Golden Girl is going so fast!
But who do you think is going to be last?

24

finish

Space Trekking

The Letterlanders have whizzed into space.
Here they all are exploring the place.
Now, a space puzzle for you and for me –
How many aliens can you see?

Pantomime Frolics

Everyone's having a fabulous time.
It's fun dressing up for the pantomime!
Can you find a dinosaur on the loose?
And who is playing Mother Goose?

Quarrelsome Queen's Questions

Can you find a picture of...

1 Annie Apple with an anchor?

2 Bouncy Ben in a barrel?

3 Clever Cat growing cabbages?

4 Dippy Duck dressed as a dinosaur?

5 Eddy Elephant exercising?

6 Firefighter Fred frying fish?

7 Golden Girl feeding geese?

8 Harry Hat Man with a hoola-hoop?

9 Impy Ink in an ink-pen car?

10 Jumping Jim jumping over a jeep?

11 Kicking King flying a kite?

12 Lucy Lamp Light posting letters?

13 Munching Mike making music?

14 Noisy Nick nibbling noodles?

15 Oscar Orange with an octopus?

16 Peter Puppy painting a picture?

17 Quarrelsome Queen with her quilt?

18 Red Robot running in a race?

19 Sammy Snake skiing in the snow?

20 Talking Tess with a telescope?

21 Uppy Umbrella upside down?

22 Vicky Violet playing the violin?

23 Walter Walrus windsurfing?

24 Fix-it Max driving a box car?

25 Yo-yo Man sailing a yacht?

26 Zig Zag Zebra zipping round a race track?

The Letterlanders

Annie Apple	Bouncy Ben	Clever Cat	Dippy Duck	Eddy Elephant	Firefighter Fred	Golden Girl

Harry Hat Man	Impy Ink	Jumping Jim	Kicking King	Lucy Lamp Light	Munching Mike

Noisy Nick	Oscar Orange	Peter Puppy	Quarrelsome Queen	Red Robot	Sammy Snake	Talking Tess

Uppy Umbrella	Vicky Violet	Walter Walrus	Fix-it Max	Yellow Yo-yo Man	Zig Zag Zebra

Letterland

Other Letterland titles for you to collect:

First alphabet activity book
Meet the Letterlanders

First reading activity book
Develop early reading skills

First handwriting activity book
Develop early handwriting skills

First rhyming activity book
Help develop reading skills

First reading flashcards

Alphabet sounds activity book
Match letters to sounds

Building words activity book
Blend letter sounds into words

Reading words activity book
Read and spell whole words

Spelling words activity book
First steps in learning to spell

Second reading flashcards

Alphabet Tales

Bedtime Stories

Fun to Find Sticker Book
Over 80 fun things to find and sticker!

First Sticker Dictionary
40 fun stickers to help you learn the alphabet!

In the Jungle / Up in Space / Under the Sea

First Picture Word Book
Trusted by parents and teachers, loved by children

An Alphabet of Rhymes

ABC
Trusted by parents and teachers, loved by children

For more information about Letterland products, please visit

www.letterland.com